Series 561

AN ADVENTURE FROM HISTORY

The Story of
CAPTAIN COOK

Written by
L. DU GARDE PEACH

Illustrated by
JOHN KENNEY

Publishers: Wills & Hepworth Ltd., Loughborough

First published 1958   ©   *Printed in England*

The Story of CAPTAIN COOK

Captain James Cook was one of the greatest of all the famous sailors who have set out from the shores of England to discover new lands.

He was born in the year 1728, in a village in Yorkshire, where his father worked on a farm. They were poor people, so very soon young James had to leave school to help his father. But he did not mean to remain a farmer, and when he was seventeen he went to work as an errand boy in a shop in Staithes, a fishing village near Whitby.

Very often he had to deliver goods down by the harbour, and it was here that he used to spend all his spare time looking at the ships and talking to the sailors. It was not long before he decided that he, too, wanted to be a sailor; before he died, he was to see more of the world than any white man had ever seen before.

The story has been told that whilst he was still an errand boy, young James Cook stole a shilling out of the till of the shop and ran away to sea. This is not true.

What really happened is that Mr. Saunderson, the man for whom he was working, wanted to help Cook. So he took him to a friend named Mr. John Walker, who owned some colliers.

These were very small ships and we may be sure that they were not very clean, because they were carrying coal up and down the east coast. But Cook did not mind that, so long as he could go to sea.

His first ship was called the "Freelove", and it was whilst sailing in her that he began to study navigation. This is a word which means the art of finding your way at sea by carefully observing the position of the sun and stars.

Mr. Walker soon heard what Cook was doing. He thought that a boy who would work in his spare time to learn how to navigate a ship was too good to be an ordinary sailor. So when Mr. Walker built a fine new ship called the "Friendship", Cook was made one of the officers.

For three years Cook sailed as mate, trading to the ports of the Baltic. This was very good training for the man who was later to sail all round the world, because the North Sea is often covered by thick fog, and a sailor has to be a good navigator to keep on course.

Cook was a very good officer, and certainly knew more about navigation than any of the other young men employed by Mr. Walker in his ships. When the Captain of the "Friendship" left, Cook was offered the post of Captain in his place. This was a fine chance for such a young man, but Cook refused. He had decided that what he really wanted to do was to join the Royal Navy.

In those days the chief way of getting sailors for the Navy was by means of what were called the Press Gangs. These were parties of officers and men who were allowed by law to go about the streets seizing men and taking them by force to become sailors in the King's ships. They also took men from the prisons; in fact there were very few sailors who had joined the Navy of their own free will.

Because these sailors were either criminals or "pressed men", as they were called, they wanted to leave the Navy as soon as they could. Cook was different. He joined the Navy because he hoped that one day he might be an officer in a King's ship.

He knew that this would not be easy, because at that time only young men with rich parents could join as officers, and Cook's father was poor. Cook believed that once he was in the Navy, his knowledge of seamanship and navigation would help him.

He was right. In less than two months he was rated as Master's Mate.

As a Master's Mate in the Royal Navy it was Cook's duty to work out the position of the ship at sea, and to give orders to the man at the wheel. It is clear that he must have been a very remarkable man to have been made responsible for the safety of a King's ship by the time he was twenty-nine.

Cook was in a ship called the "Eagle", in which he soon saw active service. War had broken out between England and France about who should have the rich new lands of Canada and Western America, and orders were given to the Navy to capture French ships wherever they could find them. In those days merchant ships were almost as heavily armed as the ships of war, and when the "Eagle" met with the French merchant ship "Duc d'Aquitaine", there was a fierce battle. A storm was raging, but because the English ship was better handled, the French vessel was captured.

Cook was now promoted to the rank of Master, and transferred to a larger ship, H.M.S. "Pembroke".

Almost immediately the English Government decided to send a strong fleet to try to take Canada from the French. One of the ships in this fleet was the "Pembroke".

If you look at a map of North America you will see a great river, the St. Lawrence, joining the five great lakes with the sea. This river runs between Canada and what is now the United States of America, but when Cook sailed in the "Pembroke", it was held by the French. The fleet had orders to sail up the St. Lawrence and hold it for England.

The expedition was successful. Some of the smaller French settlements were captured, but the most important of them, a town called Quebec, was far up the river.

The St. Lawrence is very wide and there are many islands and shallow places. Cook proved so good at finding the right channels, that when the ships had sailed up to Quebec, he was sent for by General Wolfe, who commanded the British forces.

General Wolfe had a special task for him.

The only way to attack Quebec was from the river, and to do this soldiers had to be landed from the big ships in small boats. Naturally General Wolfe wanted the ships to sail as close to the shore as possible, and Cook was told to survey the approaches.

This meant that he had to go in a small boat and find out how deep the water was, marking the shallow places on a chart.

When Cook had done this, an even more difficult task awaited him. The attack was to take place in the dark, and the soldiers were to land from small rowing boats. Cook was ordered to lead the way, and guide them through the winding channels which he had previously surveyed.

This was a very difficult thing to do in the darkness, but Cook knew that the success of the attack depended on him, and he led the way slowly and carefully.

Cook did not fail. The small boats successfully reached the beach. Before them were the cliffs known as the Heights of Abraham.

Cook's task was done, and he remained with the small boats, ready to take the soldiers back to the ships if the attack failed, but the attack did not fail.

General Wolfe and his men climbed up a steep and slippery path in the darkness and attacked the French soldiers at the top of it. More French troops charged out from the town, but the English waited until they were only forty yards away before they opened fire.

The English volley threw the French troops into confusion. Wolfe saw that this was the moment to attack. Himself leading his picked grenadiers, he charged forward.

The battle was won, but brave General Wolfe was killed at the moment of victory.

Canada now became a British possession. To-day it is, of course, a self-governing Dominion, part of the great British Commonwealth of Nations.

A more peaceful period followed. Cook had been transferred to a ship called the "Northumberland", and he had time to work at his favourite task on the St. Lawrence, the study of what is called marine surveying.

This means the making of maps of the coast of a country, as well as of the shape of the bottom of the sea near the coast. It is very important that this should be done carefully and accurately. If it is not, sailors who are steering by the maps, or charts, as they are called, can very easily be wrecked.

The making of these charts is difficult, because it is not easy to measure distances on water. But Cook taught himself how to do it, with the result that the charts he prepared were better than those made by any of the other Masters with the fleet.

The charting of the great river St. Lawrence was a task which meant long days out in a small boat, taking soundings of the depth of the water. At the same time, whenever a sounding was taken, Cook had to know where he was.

This was not easy. In many places the St. Lawrence is miles wide, and when Cook found a very shallow place or a sand-bank it was important that he should mark it in exactly the right position on the chart. This was so that ships sailing up or down the river could avoid it.

There was only one way to do this. Cook took the direction of the hills or other high points on the banks with a compass, and when he had two or more of these he was able to draw lines on the chart which gave him his position.

Day after day and month after month Cook went on patiently working out the exact position of each one of many thousands of soundings. When he had finished, his chart was so accurate that he was given a special reward by the Admiralty.

Cook was now recognised as the best man at the making of charts in the whole of the Royal Navy, so whenever new charts were required, he was ordered to prepare them.

The need soon arose. The capture of Canada had brought to England vast new territories, including the large island of Newfoundland. There were no charts of the coast of this island, so the Admiralty gave Cook the command of a ship of his own and sent him to make them. This ship, Cook's first command, was called the "Grenville".

South of Newfoundland are two small islands called St. Pierre and Miquelon. Under the peace treaty these were to be returned to France, but the British Admiralty thought it would be a good thing to have charts of them. So the French were kept waiting whilst Cook surveyed the islands and completed his charts.

The surveying of the coast of Newfoundland was difficult and dangerous. Though the island is no further north than England, the sea which surrounds it is often frozen, and is nearly always stormy.

If you again look at a map, you will see that the coast of Newfoundland is also broken by hundreds of little bays and inlets. Each of these had to be very carefully charted by Cook. He did this so well that his charts were still in use two hundred years after they were made. Only now are new ones being issued.

During the four years which it took him to make the charts of Newfoundland, Cook had many adventures. On one occasion the little boat in which he was working was upset by the carelessness of one of the sailors, and Cook was thrown into the water. He had never learnt to swim, and if a boat from one of the ships of the Navy had not been near-by, he would have drowned.

It was whilst Cook was busy making his charts of Newfoundland that a very important event happened. This was what is called an eclipse of the sun.

An eclipse of the sun is caused by the moon coming exactly between the earth and the sun, so that it is just as though the sun were blotted out of the sky. This does not happen very often, and when it does it is always very carefully observed. Parties of men are sent with special instruments to the best places from which it can be seen.

It is possible to tell beforehand when an eclipse will take place, and Cook knew that he would be able to see it on August 5th, 1766, from a little island called Burgeo, just to the south of Newfoundland.

He watched the eclipse very carefully and made some very accurate drawings of what he saw. His account and his drawings were so good that they were published by the Royal Society, a society of very learned men, originally founded by Charles II.

It was because Cook had written such a good account of the eclipse of the sun that he was sent to observe another similar event three years later. This was what is called a transit of Venus.

Venus is one of the planets which, like our earth, go round the sun. A transit of Venus is really exactly like an eclipse of the sun, except that it is Venus which is between the earth and the sun, and not the moon. Because Venus is so much further away from us than the moon, it does not blot out the sun. It appears merely as a small black dot crossing its face.

The best place from which to observe this transit of Venus was on an island called Tahiti, in the South Pacific Ocean, so Cook sailed to Tahiti in a ship named the "Endeavour".

This was to become one of the most famous ships that ever sailed out of an English Port.

Cook watched the movement of Venus across the sun and then left the island of Tahiti to carry out the second part of his instructions. This was to look for the great Southern continent which was supposed to cover the South Pole.

No one had ever been there. But from time to time sailors had seen land to the southward. They thought that this land was part of a great new continent and Cook wanted to find out whether they were right. If the southern continent did not exist, he was to sail on to New Zealand, which had already been discovered, and make a chart of the coastline and the waters surrounding it.

Cook had a map of the South Pacific on which the supposed southern continent was marked. When he had sailed his ship right across it, and found nothing but water, he went on to New Zealand.

Here he was attacked by some of the natives, called Maoris, and was obliged to fire on them in self defence. Cook always treated natives well, and it was unfortunate that he was on this occasion forced to take such action.

Cook was the first white man to sail round New Zealand. He found, as we know to-day, that it consists of two large islands, and therefore could not be part of a southern continent, as earlier sailors had thought.

Cook's orders were now to return to England, and he decided to do so by sailing round Australia, then called New Holland.

Up to this time no one had ever sailed up the eastern side of Australia. Cook decided to explore it and, as usual, to make charts of the coast.

But this coast was unlike any that he had ever seen before. A great reef of coral, called the Great Barrier Reef, stretches up the north-east coast of Australia for hundreds of miles. Cook sailed between it and the shore, but he was of course without any charts to guide him. One night, without any warning the ship struck on the reef and remained fast.

The "Endeavour" looked like becoming a total wreck.

Cook and his men were in a desperate position. They were on an unknown coast thousands of miles from home. They had no hope of rescue, for they had not seen a white man for more than a year. No one in the civilised world had any knowledge of where they were, or where to look for them if they were missing.

Cook immediately gave orders to lighten the ship by throwing overboard stores, ballast, and even some of the guns. When at last the ship floated, it was found that water was coming in fast.

There was a danger that the ship would sink, and Cook and his crew never be heard of again. But the pumps kept the water down until they could get the ship ashore. Here they stayed for a month, repairing the holes in the ship's hull.

At last they were able to sail away, but before leaving the northernmost cape of Australia, Captain Cook landed and hoisted the British flag. By doing this he claimed Australia for Britain, and it remains to-day, like Canada, a great self-governing Dominion in the British Commonwealth.

Cook arrived home with a great deal of knowledge about the Southern Ocean and the great Continent of Australia. What was, in those days, much more wonderful, he returned without having lost a single man of the crew from scurvy.

This is a sickness which people get when they have no fresh vegetables or fruit, but nobody had realised the cause, and on a long voyage as many as half the crew were expected to die from it. Captain Cook was the first man to think of a way of preventing this from happening.

Of course, he could not have fresh vegetables when the ship was out of sight of land for months. Therefore, Cook took in his ship what is called "sauerkraut", a sort of pickled vegetable.

At first the sailors would not eat it, so Cook gave orders that it was only to be served to the officers. After that all the crew wanted it, with the result that the ship sailed round the world without losing a single man from this terrible disease.

Cook was not in England for very long. A year later he was again at sea, once more searching for the great southern continent.

On this voyage Cook was absent from England for three years, and he sailed nearer to the South Pole than anyone had ever been before. Here he came to the great masses of ice and the enormous tabular icebergs of the southern ocean, and for the first time he saw penguins, the quaint and friendly birds which are found in the Antarctic.

Captain Cook's great voyage took him to within a hundred miles of the ice covered land which surrounds the South Pole. He proved that the great southern continent, which men had thought extended up into the Pacific and the Atlantic Oceans, did not exist.

Cook sailed right round the world, almost always close to the southern ice pack. It was so cold that Cook, writing about it later, said "that the sailors were often cased in frozen snow as if clad in armour".

During this voyage Cook saw and visited many of the islands in the southern seas. None of these was stranger than Easter Island.

This lonely spot of land lies far south in the Pacific Ocean. It was not actually discovered by Captain Cook. There are records of other white men who had visited it earlier in the century. None of them has ever been able to explain the very strange stone statues which are scattered all over the island.

There is nothing quite like these statues anywhere else in the world. No one knows why or when they were made, or who made them. But it is certain that the men who carved them out of the soft rock had no metal tools. Nor had they any means of moving them other than hauling them with ropes made of grass.

Some of these statues are thirty feet high and weigh fifty tons. They still remain to-day where they have stood for hundreds of years, looking out over the sea.

When Captain Cook arrived home after this long voyage, he was received with great honour. The Royal Society gave him a gold medal in recognition of his discoveries.

The King of England at that time, King George III, was very interested in travel and exploration. He received Captain Cook in his palace and questioned him closely about all that he had seen and done.

The Admiralty also recognised his services. He was promoted and made Fourth Captain of Greenwich Hospital, with a salary of £200 a year. This may not seem much to-day, but money in the eighteenth century was worth many times what it is now.

Greenwich Hospital was not what we call a hospital. It was a residence for men honoured by the country, and Cook could have lived there in comfort for the rest of his life, but this did not satisfy him. He wanted only one thing, to set out again on a voyage of discovery.

In those days men still thought that it might be possible to sail from the Atlantic Ocean round the north of Canada, into the Pacific Ocean. This was called the North West Passage, and many sailors had tried to find it, including Francis Drake.

Cook was now ordered to take two ships and find out whether such a passage existed. So he sailed southward, round the Cape of Good Hope to New Zealand, and across the Pacific Ocean to the far north-west coast of America.

No English ship had ever before sailed these waters, but Cook found some Russian sailors from eastern Siberia. He tried to find out from them whether it was possible to sail northwards.

These Russian fishermen had never heard of England, or even of Europe, and, of course, only spoke their own language. But they could draw, and they and Cook sat at a table drawing charts, from which Cook got much useful information.

Cook did not, however, discover the North West Passage. He pushed far to the northward until he was stopped by ice. In his little sailing ship he could not break through it, so he turned south again.

His intention was to spend the winter in the Hawaiian Islands and to continue his search northwards in the following spring.

When he reached this group of islands he found one, called Maui, which no one had seen before. Nor had the natives ever seen a white man, and they believed him to be the god of their tribe, by name Orono.

Nothing Cook could do or say could make them understand that he was only a man like themselves. All the time he was there he was treated like a god, with ceremonies and offerings.

But this did not prevent the natives, who were great thieves, from trying to steal anything they could from the ship.

After a month here Cook sailed away, but a storm damaged one of the ship's masts, and he returned to Maui to repair it.

He found that the natives had changed in their manner towards him and his crew. Perhaps they thought that one whose ship could be damaged by a storm could not be their god Orono. Not only were they less friendly, but they were more than ever inclined to steal from the white men.

Finally they stole the ship's cutter, one of the small boats in which the crew went ashore.

Cook landed to demand its return. Because of the unfriendly attitude of the natives, he took with him a boatload of sailors armed with muskets.

It was then that the tragedy occurred. The natives attacked Cook, and for some reason the men in the boat did not come to his help. Before he could get back to them, he was killed.

So died one of the greatest sailors and explorers England has ever known.

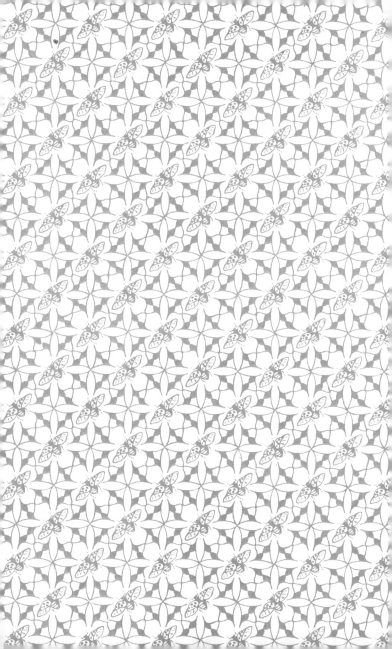